VANISHING POINT:
A CAREGIVER'S MEMOIR

_____

_____

_____

By

Evie Stiehl-Brunner

This is a personal memoir.

All names mentioned herein have been changed

except for those of immediate family, with

permission.

Also by Evie Stiehl-Brunner

The Journey (poetry)

Hardscrabble Girl (childhood memoir)

PRAISE FOR VANISHING POINT

"By putting thoughts on paper in a casual journalistic tone, Evie Stiehl-Brunner brings "Vanishing Point" into the light as a great source of comfort to all of those touched by this beautiful and intimate journey. It is an honest and respectful approach that allows the reader to observe a short period of time between diagnosis and surrender, denial and acceptance, realization and peace. Friends don't know what to say when someone is going through this difficult time. This book hears them. This book says it."

—Jessica Whiteley, B.S.
Senior Research Associate
InVentiv Clinical Solutions

"It's difficult to say what's more remarkable: The fact that Evie wrote such a beautifully detailed and thoughtful account of her last days with her father—or that she chose to share something so personal with the world."

—Chip Haskell
Creative Director
Love Advertising

"I haven't met a person as genuine and unique as Evie Brunner. The story she tells about her father is emotionally encapsulating and drives the sense of compassion and truth straight to the heart. I can relate to her story on so many levels because I too have lost a sibling years ago to tragedy. I felt my emotions stir up inside from my loss years ago as I read the heartfelt story she shared through her journal. Definitely a great story about life and learning about finding your inner strength of the Tiger, as I have through the Martial Arts."

—Aaron Faber
4th degree Black Belt
Martial Arts Instructor of Evie Brunner
United Studios of Self Defense

"In this lovely journal, Evie, with her father, relives childhood memories of their close and loving relationship. Surrounding the stories come gentle examples of support and caring through this time of farewell."

—Dale and Margaret Iverson
Iverson Family

"When a great storyteller shares a profound personal experience, you feel every emotion as though you lived through it yourself. I was deeply moved by this honest account of a father's terminal illness and the loving daughter that was left behind."

—Kelly D'Alessio
Producer
KSL Television

DEDICATION

For Dad

ACKNOWLEDGEMENTS

I want to acknowledge the people of Hospice in Salt Lake City, Utah. They were my inspiration, my hope, and my lifeline. During this most difficult time, they enabled me to appreciate the days, the hours, the moments till the final farewell.

The loving kindness of relatives and friends who kept in touch, I hold dear to my heart. I will forever be grateful to Pastor O'Donnell and others from the church for their prayers, visits, and kind assistance.

Deep gratitude and thanks to my manuscript readers Jessica Whiteley and Kelly D'Alessio.

My love and thanks to my sons Jason and Jody for their presence and strength, and to Jason for his wonderful cover photos.

Thanks to my grandson Dylan for your spirit and being, from birth, and for being with me now in karate and daily life.

Heartfelt thanks to my karate masters, Sensei Faber and Sensei Martin for their encouraging words, "Go for it, girl," both in karate and in my writing.

A special thank you goes to my friend, Diana, for her computer skills and suggestions as the project progressed.

Thanks also to Andrea who formatted the layout for publication.

Lastly, I wish to thank Tygee, the cat, my father's faithful and loving companion. He lay at Dad's side day after day, hour after hour, and howled when the end came. He knew. He stayed the course—and lost the will to live when it was over.

PREFACE

A journal can be beautiful, strange, or even difficult to believe. Months or years later one can read it and feel as though it was written yesterday. Like an ocean wave, the raw emotion of the words washes over one and leaves behind a testimony of an experience that time supposedly left behind. I have chosen to share my journal with others. It is simply the story of my father's last days after he was diagnosed with pancreatic cancer. It is the journey my father and I shared from that moment on till he left me almost four months later. Of course, it is unique and special to me.

I realize I am not alone in this experience. Many others have traveled this same journey of losing a loved one, and those who have not will most likely do so in time. It is the same journey for

9

all of us, but because we are individuals, we have
our own stories to tell, to remember, to relive,
or even at times try to forget—except we are left
behind, still breathing, forced to try to bring
meaning to the experience. And that becomes
another journey of our own making. It is my wish
that by sharing my daily thoughts and feelings
during this time, my words may bring comfort,
inspiration, or hope to others. As I reread the
journal, memories of my childhood with Daddy
invaded my thoughts, and I have chosen to include
some of these as well.

APRIL

April 1, 2004 (11:00 p.m.)

Dear Journal,

It is the end of April Fool's Day. But no one said, "April fools!" I waited all day in a sick, humorous kind of way to hear those two magic words—words that would undo the undoable. But it's going on midnight. Soon it will be too late.

Actually today isn't the true beginning. The beginning is unknown to us. Today is just the day that Dad and I became aware. He is asleep now with the aid of a sleeping pill, but I'm still going over the day. I recreate it again and again.

This morning was normal as Dad and I made conversation on the drive to the clinic for his follow-up visit and sat side by side in the private waiting room. Finally the door opened, and

Dr. Cato walked in. He said hello and then quickly moved to his chair. He opened Dad's file containing the results of his latest test. Suddenly I was overwhelmed with the need to grab Dad and run. There was something written on Dr. Cato's face, something in his manner as he rose to shake Dad's hand. Dad trusts and has faith in him, as do I.

I heard words. Dr. Cato was talking. I wanted to put a silencer between us to shut him out. And then one word jumped out from the rest, went off to the side, and hung suspended in midair—*cancer*. Dr. Cato said cancer. It hit the floor with a thud and bounced around the room like a ball with nowhere to go, floor to ceiling, wall to wall. It just kept bouncing, waiting for us to catch it. But we couldn't. We didn't want to, and even if we could have, what would we have done with it?

I'm jolted back to the present. Only a light from a small lamp touches the page as I write at Dad's small dinette in his unit at the retirement home. Dad is snoring with Tygee, his cat, snuggled at his side. One reason we selected this retirement home is because they allow pets. Tygee has been with Dad for many years. He seems to adapt to anything as long as he's with his master.

My air mattress beckons me from the floor. It has become my bed while staying nights with Dad. I must block out the day. I welcome the escape of sleep. I am overwhelmed with fatigue. Dear Journal, this is my first entry. You will be hearing from me quite often from now on. You will know the events of each day and my thoughts, feelings, and emotions. I must write. I have to. Happy April Fool's Day! There, I said it.

April 2, 2004 (10:35 p.m.)

Dear Journal,

Dad slept late. I woke at dawn and sat out on the lanai. It overlooks the grounds from his second-floor apartment. A small table and patio chair plus Tygee's litter box almost fill the small area. I could see Dad stirring through the sliding glass windows. He put on his robe and disappeared into the bathroom. His morning ritual had begun.

After he was done washing, taking his meds, and giving himself his daily injection of insulin, we sat down together for a light breakfast. Still in his bathrobe, Dad ate his usual breakfast of cereal with milk, one slice of toast with sugarless jelly, and tea. I had my usual cup of coffee. Actually by then it was probably my third or fourth cup.

Dad suggested that we not say anything to anyone in the Home about yesterday's news. His tone was matter-of-fact. He could have been talking about a news story or the weather forecast. I agreed that now wasn't the time. Then he got dressed. After a slight wave and a smile he made his way down the hall to pick up LaVerl, his lady friend.

Today was bingo day. Dad seldom misses it, and today was no exception. I stood in the open doorway as Dad left, and watched as LaVerl entered the hall, and then she and Dad disappeared into the elevator. I drove home to my condo and did my everyday routine. After grocery shopping, cleaning, and talking briefly to a neighbor, I returned to the Home around eight o'clock in the evening.

Everything was so normal, so routine; until Dad was getting ready for bed. We hugged good night, looked into each other's eyes, and burst into tears. Then very quietly, he said, "Well, I guess this is it." I nodded, but words wouldn't come. He cleared his throat and crawled into bed.

I'm out here on the lanai again, writing in the dim light from a window across the way. Day two has passed since our visit to the clinic. I'm a little perturbed, thinking that Dad is no different today than from yesterday or a week or month ago. If only he hadn't noticed that persistent pain in his lower chest and insisted on checking it out. He should have ignored it! He's the same as always. At ninety-two he's doing great! Dr. Cato was wrong. The result of the test was a mix-up. I just know Dad will be with us for a long time to come! Cancer just doesn't happen to my dad. No way! He's great actually.

April 3, 2004

Dear Journal,

It is hard to put my thoughts down on paper because I'm not sure what they are anymore. No more writing. I'm done! Everything's fine! Just fine.

April 13, 2004

Dear Journal,

The days have gone by without my writing. I guess I just didn't want to put anything down on paper. But, I must! I know Hospice is coming at three this afternoon. I wish they wouldn't. I don't want to talk with them about Dad. I guess I could cancel, pretend I'm not home. But what good would that do? They would just come back. It has to be done.

The morning went well. I cleaned my house. It seems I have extra energy these days, so I welcome the opportunity to scrub something down or vacuum something up.

I finished within an hour before my guests arrived. My house looked great. Just enough time for a quick shower and change of clothes. I was drinking a cup of coffee, which was giving me heartburn anyway, when the doorbell rang.
The Hospice people. My not-so-welcome guests had arrived.

The conversation went smoothly. It seemed that I asked the right questions, and they gave me the answers as well as they could. "Pancreatic cancer usually goes faster than eight months," Marie said, sitting next to me on the couch. The nurse sat in my reading chair. *Perhaps Dr. Cato was trying to be kind when he said eight months to a year*, I thought. *Besides, who can really know? He said he wasn't God.*

We agreed to another meeting on Thursday so Dad could meet them. I will bring him to my place. Dad is still not ready to disclose the news to the residents at the Home or the staff. We will know the right time when it comes.

I told them I would be happy to work with

them. Happy? What a strange word for a time like this. I thanked them for coming, and we stood as they prepared to leave. They hugged me, and we all smiled. But we were still sad.

Our conversation tumbled through my mind after I shut the door behind them. I recalled bits and pieces of sentences—talk about not eating toward the last, medication to administer to ease his pain, and finally an induced coma if it comes to that. Help with his personal needs. Harp music to accompany him to the other side. Help and support for me. I pride myself on being able to handle anything. I am strong. Life has taught me many things. I'll be fine. I'll do okay.

I must buy the book Marie, from Hospice, recommended about death, but I can't remember the name, even moments after she had left. I guess I'm not okay.

I am angry. *I can't do this! I just can't!*

April 23, 2004 (5:00 a.m.)

Dear Journal,

I'm at the Home. I slept well on my faithful air mattress, but I woke up at five o'clock like someone had switched on my on-off button. In an instant I was wide awake.

I haven't written anything lately. Seems like I can't put anything down. After all, what is there to say? Yes, Dad has cancer. Yes, now I truly know. It seems things are going fine with him though. Is *he* in denial?

Hospice has been here a couple of times. Dr. Cato made the arrangements. Dad seems to have mixed feelings about them, and sometimes I do too. When they walk through the door, it's like the angel of death has unexpectedly arrived. "Oh, by the way, just in case you've forgotten ... you are going to die."

I want to yell, "Stop reminding us of what is happening! Go away!" They are very nice people, but I feel they are an intrusion. Although I know they are scheduled, I resist their presence. I don't wish to talk to strangers. But it seems they want to get to know us. Hospice. What can they possibly do anyway?

Dad keeps playing bingo, visits with staff and residents, watches television, goes to the dining room, and attends the various programs. He puts one foot ahead of the other, and the days go by. It's been twenty-three days since April Fool's, and I ask myself, *What are his private thoughts?*

There are times when I just know I can fix things. I must. At the same time I'm also feeling somewhat detached from the world. I'm an outsider looking in. I'm here but someplace else at the same time. What is real, and what isn't?

I must close for now. It's six in the morning. Today is "tend grandson" day, and I have to be at my condo by eight o'clock when he arrives. Little Dylan is very real. Dad and I *need* real. I thank God for Mondays and Fridays, my tending days. The three of us plus Tygee enjoy our time together at the Home, sometimes going for short walks around the place. Dylan enjoys entertaining everyone he meets, and the residents love it. Dylan, age two, and Dad, age ninety-two, spend precious time together.

I watch with wonder.

April 24, 2004 (8:00 a.m.)

Dear Journal,

It's Saturday. I again stayed overnight. Everything is in order. I gave Dad his new medicine as the Hospice man, Todd, instructed yesterday. Dad ate his breakfast, and now he and Tygee are sleeping again. I dozed and read intermittently.

(10:45 a.m.) Just took my shower and dressed. Cup of coffee in hand, I'm on the lanai, writing. I guess it is my writing room.

The sun warms my skin and lights up the world. I gaze at the mountains—always there, dependable and strong and yet serene and comforting. My symbol of steadfast devotion as Dad and I travel this journey together. This morning I seem to see more clearly, feel more acutely. The birds are talking. The leaves are new after a long winter. The air is fresh. The sky is blue. I sense *peace*.

After feeling out of touch with myself and the world since April 1st, finally, peace settles over me, and I open myself to it. A prayer of thanksgiving goes through me and then floats heavenward. It is a good day. A good day to laugh or cry, to be happy or sad, to just *be*. The mountains echo back to me my overwhelming love for my dad, the world, God, and the universe. I am filled with it. *All* is in order. What is, *is!* I must relax into it and remain open to life, and death. I wonder if I'll feel like this tomorrow. I'm not going to give it another thought. Enjoy. Suddenly a thought races through my mind. *Dad, let's go back to the prairie. Let's go duck hunting one more time. I remember one special day.*

When I was twelve or so, my father announced that it was time I learned how to handle guns. He set up empty cans, sometimes in the yard, other times in the south pasture, where we spent hours practicing. At first I wasn't really sure

I wanted to learn, but as time passed, it became a big challenge.

He explained how to sight in a gun, how to pull the trigger slowly, gently, and how I was not to shut my eyes as the gun went off. The cans went skipping across the dirt, making music as I hit each one. I aimed at a particular shape on the can, and when I finished, we gathered them up to see how close I came to my mark. Surprisingly, as time passed, I hit the mark more and more. My father said I was good with a gun, and that made me feel great.

After I had aimed at cans for a period of time, it was time to go on to bigger things. Dad took string, tied a coffee can to the end, and threw it in the air over the electrical lines. As it swung back and forth, I practiced hitting a moving target. It took a while, but eventually I grew skillful enough to hit my mark as it moved through the air.

My first gun was a BB gun, and I ran around the yard aiming at everything in sight that looked like a good target. Though I could never bring myself to shoot at a living creature, I became a good shot and felt confident that if I ever, by some strange reason, had to shoot an animal or a person, I could hit my mark. Somehow it seemed right that I could.

One afternoon my dad announced we were going to go duck hunting in the north pasture. I had never been duck hunting with my father before and wasn't sure I really wanted to. But because he seemed so intent on the whole affair, I went along with it. Maybe it will be fun, I thought to myself as we started off to the pasture, the gun perched between us against the seat of the pickup.

It was a warm autumn day. Billowy clouds made large round shadows across the prairie as we drove into the hills of the pasture. We headed for the dam, the perfect place to scare up some ducks. We parked a short distance away. Dad started ahead of me, leading the way, the gun slung over his shoulder. I followed in his footsteps. Time seemed to stand still. We kept walking. Suddenly Dad crouched down. He began to crawl, hugging the ground as he moved ahead of me. It looked pretty silly to me, but I decided that this was how to duck hunt, so I crouched down and began to crawl a short way behind.

He turned to look at me. "Shhh," he said, his finger poised across his lips. I knew we were approaching the dam below the ridge ahead of us. We had to be extra quiet at this moment so he could take careful aim without scaring the ducks away.

We crawled slowly, our movements very deliberate so as not to make the slightest noise and alert the ducks to our presence. So this is how the Indians did it, I thought to myself as I watched my father's foot staring me in the face.

We were there. My father rose up, his gun aimed, finger on the trigger. Ducks! Where were the ducks? The dam was there in the quietness of the day, the water motionless. Not a duck in sight. Nothing moved on the water!

It was all for nothing! I fell over laughing, especially when I saw my father's expression as he peered over the ridge. I lay on the ground, feeling its warmth against my back, laughing at the surprised look on my father's face. I couldn't stop.

My father laughed too but not nearly as much as I did. He didn't seem to think it was quite so funny.

April 25, 2004 (7:00 p.m. on Sunday)

Dear Journal,

Slept in. I can sleep, thank God. Drove to the condo around noon. Checked on my cat, Mamma Kitty, and watched television for an hour or so. Left my condo and picked up Dad and then went for a drive up Millcreek Canyon. Dad seemed to enjoy it. I had a feeling of irritability settle under my skin. I wouldn't allow myself to wonder why. Jean called in the evening. It's always nice to hear the voice of a friend.

She can empathize, as she lost both of her parents to cancer. I have a new understanding of her struggle as well. After I hung up the phone, I was suddenly aware of how tired I had been. I'm overwhelmed with tiredness. I'm an awake-tired me these days. Dad is sleeping.

April 26, 2004 (Monday)

Dear Journal,

After a fast shower I dressed quickly. I'm running behind, as I must be at the condo for Dylan by 8:00. Tygee blinked at me a couple of times and poked his nose against Dad's neck as he slept. Then he did a giant stretch before he jumped off the bed and moved to his breakfast dish. I slipped quietly out the door with a whispered good-bye to him and Dad. No reason to wake him.

27

Dylan's mom and I arrived at the condo at the same time. Dylan's sweet smile warmed me as we made our way into the condo. Later while Dylan took his afternoon nap, I relaxed on the couch. Everything was quiet. I tried to read with Mamma Kitty curled up next to me, purring her little heart out. I've spent so little time with her as of late. But I couldn't concentrate. The words blurred and slid off the page.

It would be so nice to have Mom here, right now, this very minute. She left us too soon. Christmas has never been the same, as she died on Christmas morning of 1976. Lung cancer. Dad was always telling her to throw away the cancer sticks. A quick calculation in my head tells me it's been almost thirty years now. Unbelievable. I hated the holiday after that. But I made the best of being the only female left to make Christmas joyous for the family from then on, but it was hard. I missed her while making lefse, preparing turkey, last-minute shopping, and wrapping presents.

Mostly I missed the chatter, the busyness, the bonding, and the sharing. Mothers and daughters need each other to make things fun, to make the world go round. "Mom, if only we could chat," I whispered into the empty space in my heart. And then the tears came. *What am I mourning now?* I asked myself, reaching for a tissue buried deep in my jean pocket. The loss of my mom? The loss of my cousin, Sherrie, who was like a sister to me? The loss of my marriage? The loss of my dream of living happily ever after? My mourning covered the past, the present, and what was to come all rolled into one.

Mom made it to sixty-five when I was thirty-five. The boys were six and ten. Sherrie died at age thirty-six. My marriage died I'm not sure at what age. Maybe it never had a birth. Time to eat a snack. When Dylan wakes up, we will go to the Home and spend part of the day with Dad. I called around two, and he was on his way to an afternoon program. He lives each day fully, and so must I. Is there a right way to do this cancer thing?

Dear Journal, the one thing I've been so aware of today is that I *miss* my mom. Dad and I don't talk about her much anymore. Perhaps too many years have gone by. What is there to say? I talk about her with my aunts though. A girl thing, I guess.

MAY

May 1, 2004 (8:15 p.m.)

Dear Journal,

Thirty-one days! One month ago today we were sitting in Dr. Cato's office, receiving the news! I can still visualize the ball I saw so clearly that day. I haven't caught it yet. I don't think Dad has either. However, I see the bouncing is slowing down a bit, not so wild and out of control. Maybe we could catch it now if we tried, but still we don't want to. The time is coming when it will stop bouncing, and without even realizing the exact moment, we will hold it in our hands. We will feel its weight, its color, its texture. We will know the ball's nature, and it will become a part of us.

This last month, although all seems normal on the outside, has been filled with conflicting emotions. Unexpressed feelings of confusion, adjustment, resignation, and sadness lie hidden in the closet of my mind. Crazy how it works—back and forth from one feeling to another without one feeling in particular settling in. A roller coaster— that's what it is. Is Dad feeling this too? Maybe we should talk about the ball. But we don't.

April is really over. That's good. That's bad. We've gained and lost precious time, depending on how one looks at it. Hospice is still with us. Once a week someone with Hospice comes by. After a brief examination, a few questions, and some kind smiles, they leave. "Call if you need us."

Yes, Hospice came at Dr. Cato's suggestion, and we gave our consent. It just seems too soon. Dad and I are handling things our way. Aren't we? I should read the literature they left me. The Home staff tells me wonderful things about Hospice. Yeah, dear Journal, the staff here now knows of Dad's condition but not the residents. Hospice people don't look any different than anyone else, so residents look upon them as visitors when they enter the lobby. Or I like to think so. One thing about this retirement home situation is that it's like a big family. Everyone or someone is always watching, looking, talking, or checking out someone else. I'm tempted to tell Sue, a resident I've grown fond of, but I won't. Not yet.

Dad is about to return from a concert downstairs in the entertainment room. I must say they have good entertainment here. I hear muffled voices in the hallway. I know Dad is approaching because of the expression on Tygee's face. Cats *do* have expressions, you know. Dad's presence suddenly seems to fill the room. He grabs a cup from the cupboard and fills it with water and moves toward the microwave. Time for his last cup of tea for the day.

May 2, 2004 (9:06 p.m. on Sunday)

Dear Journal,

Dad and I went to a morning church service downstairs. Dad and LaVerl, his lady friend, spent the day together with her family. My friend Verona

called. "Let's scrapbook if you can get away."
The timing was perfect. How did she know? God
is good.

Somewhere along the way—I don't
remember the day—I told her about Dad. I knew
she sensed something all along. We can't keep this
to ourselves forever. It's mostly LaVerl we want to
protect, as we don't know how she will react. She
seems to get upset more easily lately. Why put this
burden on her before we have to?

Verona is one of my Hawaii-trip friends.
Actually we've know each other for years. We met
in church when I was a new member. In 1999, five
of us church lady friends decided to vacation in
Waikiki. Afterward, three of us met at Verona's
once a week to scrapbook our adventure. And today
she called … to scrapbook again. If she planned this
to get me out of the house, I am grateful. Dad's
apartment, my home, Dad and the boys, and the
everyday chores of living and caring take up my
time. My world is shrinking.

I'm scrapbooking my grandson starting today. Can one think of anything else while being creative? Colors, shapes, photographs, and other paraphernalia only known to the scrapbooking world surround us from wall shelves to our working area. "Does it look nice this way or that?" was an often asked question, and we gave our advice and opinions to one another gladly.

Now I'm back home again, my condo this time. I am going over the day. I am so aware of how I felt today. Freedom and escape are two words that come to mind. But of course, I wasn't really free. I called LaVerl's daughter to see if all was going well with LaVerl. And I just talked with Dad. He's in bed now. Said he had a nice day, but he is extremely tired. I can hear it in his voice.

"See you tomorrow," he says. My real bed feels warm and comforting as I finish this day's entry. Mamma Kitty is so pleased to have things so normal once again. She settles into a comfortable position across my midsection. All is normal. I like to think so anyway.

May 4, 2004 (11:00 a.m.)

Dear Journal,

Another program is going on downstairs for the residents. But Dad isn't going, even though LaVerl just called.

He's changing. The events and weekly activities no longer seem as inviting to him. He seems to want to sleep more and spend more time in his apartment. Maybe that is his escape, his refuge. He doesn't discuss his personal feelings. Maybe he will later. I'll just have to wait till he's ready. We are going to have lunch in his room as he doesn't feel like going to the dining area. He also isn't so excited about food these days. Dad always loved to eat. I remember a comment from Auntie Bobby from years ago. She is gone now. "I like to have Hienei over for dinner. He eats whatever I cook like he just loves it. Each and every bite!"

I remember how my mom would give me a spoonful of macaroni to give to him as it was boiling to see if it was done. He was our true tester. "Hmmm, a few minutes more, but don't overdo it," he would say. To this day I can't believe that Mom couldn't tell. I think it was for my benefit and maybe Daddy's too.

Anyway, Dad is taking a shower, and I must set the table. Bye for now.

May 6, 2004 (Midnight on Thursday)

Dear Journal,

I just carried my journal to the lanai so I can write. Fell asleep unexpectedly while I was watching the news. Dad and Tygee sleep peacefully. Of course, Tygee didn't need a sleeping pill, but Dad did. I wake up sometimes with a feeling of panic, and tonight is one of those nights. I can't identify the reason. It's a visitor I cannot control, and so I deal with it by sneaking onto the lanai with a glass of milk and a treat. I watch the moon, feel the night air, or count stars. It goes away, thank God, but then I'm left with worries about our farm so far away, what lies ahead, the boys, and who knows what. Things always seem worse in the middle of the night.

My boys stop by often, offer support, and love to share time with their grandpa. But losing a grandparent is not the same as a child losing a father or mother. Cousin Joyce told me that after her mom's death, she actually felt like an orphan. I understand now. We cousins are next in line. For some weird reason I feel like it is a responsibility or a calling. In the game of life we are now *it*.

Mom left us so quickly with no time for her or us to prepare. Maybe we were lucky. Which is better? Fast or slow? Of course, Dad and I grieved her passing, but I was in denial and didn't know it. I went back to a part-time office job after I went home to the farm cemetery for the funeral and actually took pride in the fact that I was handling everything so well—that is, till I returned to the farm later that summer. The wildflowers bordering the front of the house, which were usually well-groomed, were neglected and forlorn.

In that instant I realized how unattended and alone I had been feeling. The flowers would never again feel Mom's touch. And neither would I.

I know she went through suffering when her dad died of stomach cancer. I was about one year old. Then when Grandma died, she cried for what seemed a whole second as she told me the news. Then just as quickly, the sobbing stopped, and I never heard her cry again. I was about ten and had a brief moment of surprise when I heard her crying. After all, she was the stoic one, the strong, silent Norwegian.

With no siblings, I face this alone. What's so great about being an only child? It's lonely at times with no one to remember this or that. Maybe I will organize a club for children with no siblings. Dad is stirring, Journal. I'm going to offer him noodle soup, our favorite. We eat whenever we want to, and that's good. Sometimes he awakens in the middle of the night as well. He says nothing of feeling any panic though. He just says he is wide awake and wants to eat. It's actually an old habit.

Perhaps it stems from having diabetes. He eats smaller amounts but gets hungry a short time later. This time the sleeping pill didn't work

through the night. Anyway Journal, it's time
to eat.

May 12, 2004 (Wednesday)

Dear Journal,

Time passes. I seem not to remember what
has happened in what order since my last entry six
days ago. The weeks go by. Between taking care
of Dad and Dylan and the daily activities of life, I
keep busy. The boys call and check often.

During spare moments I busy myself with
my condo. I rearrange pictures and furniture. Then
I work on Dad's apartment. Maybe if I change
things, things will change. But if not, changing my
surroundings and his makes me feel as if I have
control over something.

We spent Mother's Day with Jody and
Jeanette at his house. We talked, laughed, and
enjoyed our barbeque. I sat next to Dad and
suddenly realized that this would be the last
Mother's Day we would share with him. The

thought of it settles in the pit of my stomach. I turned my thoughts elsewhere.

May 15, 2004 (6:30 p.m.)

Dear Journal,

I've been unwilling to write over the last few days. No reason exactly. Just didn't feel like it. What's the use? Will I ever want to read it anyway? Who cares?

Today, though, I'm writing because of a dream I had last night. Perhaps when I read this account of it someday, its meaning will come to me. In the dream I'm in the backseat of a car, sitting behind the driver's seat. The only thing is that there is no driver. I'm alone. The car is rolling over and over. It seems there has been an accident, but I know the details don't matter. It's me in the car that's the important thing. At first I'm very frightened. The car continues to turn over and over. I have to protect myself somehow so I won't be hurt. Then suddenly my attention is drawn to the car. It seems very important that I concentrate. The interior is gold and familiar to me. (Shades of gold and yellow have always been my favorite.) But this is a gold that is indescribable. It has energy and power in it. It radiates warmth and goodness. It is like the gold of God. It penetrates into my very being. I see two crossbars across its roof made of solid gold. I am comforted by knowing that they are there to protect me. I feel warm, safe, and secure as I roll over and over along with the car. A peace beyond understanding washes over me. I relax into the movement of the car with full knowledge that I will survive.

They say dreams tell us something we want or need to know. Right now I can't think that hard. Maybe later.

Today was a very ordinary, unordinary day much like the day before and I imagine the day to come. Dad and I drift through the days. Are we living? All that matters is that we are together, whatever we are doing.

May 18, 2004 (10:00 p.m. on Tuesday)

Dear Journal,

Meant to write yesterday. Kept thinking about it. Night came. I crawled into bed and said, "To hell with it." Maybe also I haven't written because I had a bad day. Nothing in particular made it that way. Guess it was the mood I was in. But I did have Dylan to keep me company. He is always a joy. That little man is, as they say, "the light of my life." Interesting that at this time of my life my time is taken up by an old man and a very young one. They occupy not only my time but my thoughts and prayers as well.

Now I wonder why it is that I was so irritable yesterday. One of those days when I was just looking for a fight. The checker at the grocery store didn't look right. The guy who innocently said hello to me made me mad. Family and friends weren't paying enough attention, and the sun didn't shine the way it should. Not to mention that the sky was falling. (Well, it looked like it anyway.) I wrapped myself up with all this negativity, and Dad somehow got lost in the shuffle. Writing about it today makes me feel like an idiot. I somehow mentally blocked him out of my mind most of the day. Dylan at least was a distraction for a while. We visited Dad for an hour or so, and then I took Dylan home.

While I went to the pharmacy around seven to pick up Dad's pills and insulin, I kept thinking of what color to paint my bedroom. Where did that come from? A day ago I loved the room just as it was. Now, God, those pills. I think he takes about eleven daily now. Can that really be necessary? But faithfully, he takes them as though somehow they will change things. The pharmacy was out of insulin and the nose spray that he wanted. Out? So I would have to go back in a day or two. I wanted to strike out at the pharmacist, and I knew he knew it, which made me feel really good.

Dad and I spent the evening watching television, same old, same old. Why can't the news be pleasant at least once? We went to bed around eleven, and then we had noodle soup around one in the morning. I noticed that as Dad shuffled sleepily from his bed to the table, how frail he was. It brought me to my knees. I wanted to cry, but instead I hugged him. Silently I apologized to God for my stinkin' attitude all day. Then Dad and I about fell into our separate beds. I think I got to sheep number twenty-four, and then I was out.

Looking at it today, what a relief sleep offered. I have no explanation as to why I was so irritable all day. Testy, mean, and short-tempered— that was me all through the day. Looking back now, I was just plain angry all day long.

May 19, 2004

Dear Journal again,

Left Dad around ten after breakfast of toast and juice. He is eating so little these days. Of course, we checked his sugar and made sure he took his pills. Then I left him watching television and knew he would drift back to sleep.

I headed home to my condo and my cat. Out

of the blue I stopped at Home Depot to buy white paint for my patio fence. So I then spent all of today painting! It looks very nice, Journal. But I did some thinking as I applied the paint strokes, and I came to this conclusion. This is just busy work. The fence wasn't in great need of paint when I actually examined it. But after yesterday I wanted this day to be a normal, everyday day. Painting would do it. Physical labor would do it. So I did it! Of course, I called Dad a couple of times.

And of course, I made another trek to Wal-Mart for insulin and nose spray. This time they had it. The girl who waited on me had the hiccups. Strangely it made me laugh heartily. Maybe I overdid it a bit. The pharmacist and I know each other very well after all these pill runs. Since I've ordered three thousand dollars' worth of pills during the last year, I feel we are good friends! Dad mentioned today that he feels pain in his chest. Not like a heart pain though. Todd from Hospice was here and prescribed pain medication. Another pill to pick up. Up to now Dad has only been using

Tylenol for any discomfort he feels. None of us said the word, but we were thinking it. He is beginning to have pain now. Today he asked me to replenish his vitamin supply, and he also paid his yearly dues to the NRA.

Life goes on. Life is normal. At this moment I admire my dad for simply going on. One step ahead of the other. The hard days are ahead, but until you get there, it's just a big open territory just waiting to be explored. I'll ask him sometimes how he is feeling. He just smiles slightly and says something like, "Life goes on. Such as it is." I'll say something like, "It's been a pretty good day, huh?" Time for bed.

May 22, 2004 (1:00 a.m.)

Dear Journal,

I can't do this anymore! This morning dad was zombie-like, really out of it. I think the pain medicine Hospice prescribed did it. No more of those till he truly needs it. He said so himself. He said when he first woke up and went into the bathroom, he couldn't put things together in his mind. He said he was all "flubbed up." Later we found his blood pressure medicine in his pocket after he searched for about an hour. Now that I think about it, he is more confused these days.

How can one stay *normal* under these circumstances? Knowing you are dying? Sometimes I wonder if it would have been better *not* to know till right toward the end. What good does it do either of us to carry around this knowledge, and what do we do with it? I feel a thousand years old even with a good night's rest. And Dad is turning into skin and bones.

Sometimes he just sits in his chair, scratching his head, and stares at the floor for what seems like an endless amount of time. Drives me nuts. Then I ask myself if I should ask him questions about dying, but I don't. He still doesn't talk about it, but Dad is like that. What is there to say about dying. You just do it.

My friend Martha called while she was standing in line to buy Rod Stewart tickets, asked me to go. I accepted, of course. Although it is a few months away. The outside world enters in sometimes, but mostly I feel like I'm in a box I can't climb out of. Only time will get me out, and I don't want out anyway because I know what that means. I'm in my lanai writing room with the trusty street lamp. The night is cool, and the light breeze is comforting. I should cry sometime, really hard, but I don't. Not sure why.

May 23, 2004

Dear Journal,

Can you believe it! I actually left Salt Lake City today. A friend from Hawaii was here visiting relatives, and I drove to Ogden to see him. I actually drove thirty miles and got out of town for about six hours. The staff at the Home checked on Dad. They delivered his dinner to his room so he didn't have to go down to the dining area. It is getting to be an effort, and I really don't think he wishes to converse much with anyone, including the staff. I arrived back at the Home about eight and helped him get

49

ready for bed. He asked me three times if he had taken his pills. You know, something is truly different now. What could have happened in the last day or two? That one pill?

He is asleep now, and I'm on the lanai. The drive today was a reminder that there is a world that is going on other than my little one. I'll be happy to be back in that world again. Actually, no, I won't be, because then I won't have Dad. Either/or, one or the other—I just have to go with the flow. No arguing or complaining, just acceptance. It is so hard!

May 24, 2004 (8:30 a.m. on Sunday)

Dear Journal,

Gave Dad his pills, tested his sugar, and he is now eating toast and juice. He prefers to eat sitting on the edge of his bed now, and he uses his nightstand as his table. An outsider would be shocked to see how thin he is. For me it's been a gradual thing, so I'm accustomed to it, I guess. At certain moments, though, it really hits home with me too. He said he has no pain today, but he has very little appetite anymore. Food doesn't taste good, he says. But he eats anyway.

Well, I fed him, Tygee, and myself, so we're all happy. We're fed anyway. Soon Dad will crawl under the covers again and go to sleep. I will head to the condo to see my cat and check things out there. Busyness is good. More later.

(10:25 p.m.) Who would take my place? I ask myself. I wish someone would. Is it really good to be needed? I wish no one needed me at the moment, not even me.

I feel like I've gone someplace strange in my head and can't find my way home. But my body functions fine. I clean. I eat. I take care of business, and keep taking care of business. And I keep busy.

May 25, 2004 (9:25 p.m. on Tuesday)

Dear Journal,

I'm so grateful that today I could appreciate the day. My world is chaos, but I could see beauty in it all. Don't know what made the difference. I'm just happy to be alive, happy to have Dad alive, and grateful for my boys, grandson, and my life in general. I sat out on the lanai in the wee hours of the morning and listened to the chirping of birds, the early hum of traffic, and the sound of leaves rustling in the breeze.

A plane flew over. Sounded like a transport plane, as it made more noise than usual. I always wonder where airplanes are headed. Where are the people going, and do they feel free? That's how Dad said he felt while he was flying his private plane—free from the earthbound business of living and doing. I remember the times I went flying with him at our farm. He taught me how to fly the plane around in a circle. I actually got the hang of it. He seemed proud of me. With his diabetes, he hasn't flown now for a long time. I know that must have been hard. He didn't say much. He just stated the fact that his flying days were over.

Dylan spent part of the day with me at the condo. It was a quiet, delightful day. My grandson has a way of making things normal. I go from moment to moment, lost in his presence. These days he is a special blessing to Dad and me when he spends the day. Thank God we share this special time together.

Dad told me he woke up in the night. I usually make him noodle soup when he wakes up in the middle of the night. This time I was so tired that I didn't hear him. I told him to wake me the next time. Jean called me today just to say hello. It gave me some comfort to share with her, as she still feels the loss of both her parents. I guess one learns to live with it. These days friends are very special as are my cousins. My boys visit Dad and do as well as they can. He loves to see them. Sometimes they play checkers, but he is not really up to that anymore. I have spurts of anger these days at my parents for having only me.

But it had to be that way, I was told. I was lucky or blessed to come out okay being born almost three months early. It would be so nice to have a sibling to share and talk over each day's changes and challenges concerning Dad, someone who shares your family history. You make do with what you have though. Now I will allow myself to cry a little. I really should. Crying is good for the soul. Dad, let's fly away to nowhere! *I recall so clearly his happy days of flying.*

One day Dad announced quite casually that he was "going to learn to fly." Off we went to town two days later, drove to the small airport, parked the car near the hangar, and then he disappeared inside. Mom and I sat waiting for what seemed forever. Returning, he was all smiles as he started the car.

"Next week I start," he said eagerly. "My instructor is Winn! I like him."

So began our twenty-five-mile weekly drives to his beloved new adventure. As Mom and I sat waiting in the airport's waiting area, we watched through the window his practice takeoffs and landings. Then some months later came the big day! He had earned his license. But first came his solo flight of some distance. He planned thoroughly and carefully with much anticipation and some nervousness. Once it was over, he was grinning and almost dancing. My dad?

Later he bought his first plane. A yellow cloth Funk. A new way of life had entered our small world. Of course, the plane needed a home, so a hangar was added to an outbuilding facing the new runway.

He would often say during our many flights together that while he was flying, he felt truly free. And if he had not lost one eye, he would have tried

for the US Air Force! Really? He was always a farmer to me. Many new flying experiences were added to his life personally as well as experiences with his family and friends. Amazing how much an airplane and a pilot can add to daily farm life. From checking cattle in the south pasture to flying to air shows, to flying to far-off destinations with his brother, Carl, and other pilots, Dad was a happy man.

May 27, 2004 (10:30 p.m. on Thursday)

Dear Journal,

The morning ritual changed today. Rather than toast, Dad had cereal and milk. And he again sat at the table. He said he had a burning in his stomach, so I thought maybe orange juice wasn't the best choice. His blood sugar was 213. The doctor reduced his insulin dose because of his loss of weight. Actually Dad had an appointment with the doctor yesterday. Partly why I haven't written. Anyway, he now weighs 120 pounds, and it will continue to go down. Dr. Cato's words of wisdom tell us that infection or pneumonia could get him before the cancer. Or a heart attack is possible. If I have a choice, I would hope for the heart attack. It seems to be the easiest one to deal with. Like *who* has a choice?

Everything was going as expected under the circumstances, we were told. We did make another appointment for the end of August, but I just felt that Dr. Cato didn't believe he would actually see us then.

Dad was so quiet after our visit. I wondered if we should have even bothered. What must it feel like to get a death sentence, and with this visit, it suddenly became very real—a death sentence. We just don't know the date of the execution. I am so angry. At least a prisoner, for good or bad, has that knowledge.

Dad keeps plugging along. He just wants family to talk with, eat with, be with. Last night we had a midnight snack, noodle soup once again! He still manages to eat now and then in the dining room with LaVerl.

It poured rain today. Just to match my mood? Out on the lanai I didn't hear the familiar chirping of birds. I guess birds don't sing in the rain. Only Gene Kelly does that. It's like the earth is taking a much-needed drink. That's what I need—a big, long, refreshing drink.

May 29, 2004 (11:00 p.m. on Saturday)

Dear Journal,

I took two aspirin last night to sleep. Morning went as usual. Same ritual of pills and breakfast. In the afternoon we had a big downpour. Around 7:00 p.m. Dad and LaVerl went down to the grand lounge to be entertained by John, a resident with a beautiful singing voice. I sneaked in behind them.

Afterward I accompanied them both to the second floor, where they separated. Dad mentioned that he was feeling pain in his lower back and stomach area. After he took a pain pill, he went quickly to sleep. Later I checked in on LaVerl and saw that she had on her oxygen, as her daughter told me she tends to forget it sometimes. She was very depressed. She is now in the early stages of Alzheimer's, but I have a distinct feeling that she is aware of how sick Dad truly is. She kept asking if Dad was all right. I told her Dad was just extra tired and tucked her in bed. She has been good for him. They shared many happy moments together, for which I'm grateful. At first, I admit, I was not sure I wanted to share Dad with her but realized I was acting like a selfish child. She is a good woman. The timing of this is so strange. She is leaving us bit by bit with her mind, and for Dad it is with his body.

LaVerl's daughter, Nicole, and I agreed not to tell her the true nature of Dad's illness because she would become too upset. It was hard to tell Nicole, as their family had included Dad in their activities. Actually I had gone on a long ride with them myself to Delta, LaVerl's hometown.

I am grateful that Dad had some female companionship during his later phase of life. I think there is sometimes talk when two old folks meet and fall in love. Maybe a snicker here and there even. I have learned so much over the years about being old. The needs and wants of the elderly remain the same as everyone's. There is sometimes a need to connect with a special someone, and *if* that happens, it is a blessing.

I just think that inside every so-called old person is a young person. Only time has covered him/her with a blanket, and we don't bother to look under the covers to see who is still there. Even for those who have seemingly lost it, there is a person behind the eyes if you take the time to really look. The soul shines through *if* we just look for it.

JUNE

June 3, 2004 (Thursday)

Dear Journal,

We made it to June. Two months ago since that unfunny April Fool's joke. I don't like April Fool's Day anymore—that's for sure.

Speaking of animals knowing the truth about their master, Tygee now sits like a guard dog next to Dad's head as he lays on the pillow. I'm sure he knows, watching, meowing, as if to say, "Do something." He is old now too and is hard of hearing just like his master. Such a faithful little cat Tygee is—and a very loving one. Whenever Hospice arrives to check on Dad, Tygee is right in the middle of it. How many years have they been together? Forever it seems. Tygee was left in our neighborhood while we lived in the suburbs. One

day, Thanksgiving Day to be exact, there he was—
just a kitten searching for a home, sitting in our
driveway, snowflakes drifting over him. I left him,
as I was on my way to a Thanksgiving celebration.
Upon my return the driveway was empty. I walked
into the house, heard a pitiful meow, and there he
was, staring at me through the sliding glass doors
that led to the patio. I brought him into the house,
of course.

When Dad later drove to Utah to spend the
Christmas holiday with us, we decided to give him
the kitten as a special gift. We kept him hidden in
the garage. On Christmas Eve we tied a red ribbon
around his neck, and he curled up into a little ball in
the guest room bed and fell asleep. Later we led
Dad into the room, blindfolded him, and presented
him with his new pet. I don't recall who named him
Tygee. I guess Dad did somewhere along the way.
Anyway, they loved each other from that moment
on. They had many happy moments while on the
farm. We always wanted Tygee to tell us where he
came from, but he decided to keep it a secret. Or

since he was so young, he couldn't remember.

The last few days have been a little harder than usual. Dad had a reaction to a different pain medication and was nauseous over the Memorial Day weekend. Hospice man, Todd, came by with another medicine, but he stayed sick all day. Jason, Jody, and Dylan spent Memorial Day with us at Dad's apartment, and it was a good time in spite of him not feeling his best.

But now I notice that he seems to want his pain medication plus sleeping pills at night. The doctor is considering a steroid, which will supposedly have a more positive effect on him. It might improve his appetite and rev him up a bit. Hospice will deliver it shortly.

Last evening I spent in the dining hall with Sue, my good resident friend, until the wee hours of the morning. Talking and laughing, just girl talk. We have become close over the time Dad has been here. John, the local resident singer, has become a friend as well. Upon Dad's arrival here, we assumed they were members of the staff since they were younger and just didn't fit the picture of most of the residents. Of course, they have their stories to tell of how and why they are here. Aren't we all stories after all?

We are moving into a hot spell after some rainy days. The flowers I planted for dad are growing like crazy in a terracotta pot sitting on his lanai. Actually I probably planted them for me, as Dad does not come onto the lanai these days.

Memories come flooding back of my mother's struggle to grow flowers on the farm. She always tried to create beauty around her.

Dad and I actually went for a drive today. The preparation seems to take longer than the journey itself. But Dad is not himself today. He lost his balance a couple of times, and his speech is very slow and slurred. Oh dear, it must be the magic of drugs. What would we do without them? Things can be so funny sometimes. We stopped at McDonald's to pick up to-go hamburgers.

From there we drove to a city park to eat in the beautiful outdoors. While I carry the burgers and our drinks plus his oxygen tank, I notice out of the corner of my eye that he is swaying a bit unsteadily as he walks ahead of me to the tree I'm pointing at. For some strange reason I stifle a laugh. This is funny? His growing unsteadiness and yet strong determination to find a good spot to enjoy our burgers contradicts my ease of movement. The strong and the weak—that's us doing our best to make everything seem normal.

It is very difficult now for him to lower his body to a sitting position under the tree. At this very moment I truly realize how frail he has become. We happen to be on an incline in the shade of the tree, and he sits down, propping himself firmly against the trunk to eat. But somehow he keeps falling to the side as he eats. Just changing his position without thinking about it is a thing of the past. I struggle to help him from sliding down the small incline, but he keeps sliding. By now I am laughing at the hopelessness of the situation, and yet mostly I want to scream. His expression is so funny. It's like, "What the hell is wrong here?" Finally he leans against me as we finish eating. Then he lays flat on the ground, using my lap as a pillow.

We are silent. The seagulls fly by searching for leftover French fries or scraps of burgers. The flies buzz, and children's laughter drifts to us from a far-off place. Dad makes comments about the clear blue sky and how it reminds him of the sky over the farm. The exact words I do not remember. It was too sad. I know he longs for it. Finally we manage to make it back to my jeep. I help him in, oxygen tank and all, and off we go. At least he enjoyed the outdoors for a while. He is not at all capable today. Maybe the medicine is working because he is feeling no pain ... and not much of anything else either—like his feelings perhaps.

June 5, 2004 (Saturday)

Dear Journal,

Dad finished his juice and cereal from bed and is now asleep again. I've said this before, but this time it really is different. Dad truly is different now. Everything is in slow motion. He's forgetting the time of day and what pills he has taken. He lacks interest in anything ranging from watching television to participating in the Home's activities. He also tells me that spending time with LaVerl is too difficult, and he has stayed away from her for a time. He wonders if she should be moved into a facility where she can get more attention and care. She can no longer be a companion, as it appears she may have some dementia, and he is unable to help her care for her needs, which he did for a while. So many things are coming to an end, including their special relationship. I tell myself that I'm into the acceptance stage of what's happening. If he went today, I would be happy for him. That's what I tell myself anyway.

He will never again be a part of the activities at the Home. Nothing will be enjoyable again. Nothing really matters. Any real quality of life is over. When did it actually happen? How could I not see the exact moment when he left part of him behind? What's left? Time, I guess. Just time. Suddenly I realize that I must take him home with me to the condo. We will live together there till the end. No more traveling back and forth for me, no more cleaning his apartment. I cleaned it so well and often the maid didn't have to. It was probably the cleanest apartment in the place. I should have gotten a medal! Cleaning was my release.

Mentally I've made a decision to move Dad, but tomorrow I will take the proper steps to carry it through. In the middle of the night, I actually cleaned out the shelves of his bathroom as he slept. Then unexpectedly I began to discard items either unused or useless or never to be used again.

Cleaning was my first step of the move, but I didn't realize it at the time.

This move will be good, I tell myself. *We can go for walks around the grounds of my condo. Rather, I will push him around in a wheelchair. Or should I take him home to the farm?* I ponder that.

But I need the comfort of knowing the boys are near. I need to know his doctor is close by. I have come to rely on the people of Hospice for advice and suggestions plus their care of Dad, and I will need them even more, I realize. And I need the happiness that Dylan brings into this gloomy picture. How can I start over at the farm now that the ball is rolling downhill? The thousand-mile trip home seems endless now. I weigh the positives and negatives over and over again. I cry! I should have done it sooner, if it was to happen at all. But when could I have done it? I didn't know it would be like this. I thought I would have time.

I am simply overwhelmed by everything. I can't think anymore. Not today.

Evie Stiehl-Brunner   Vanishing Point: A Caregiver's Memoir

June 6, 2004 (Sunday)

Dear Journal,

Our morning ritual was late this morning. Too much going on inside my head, so I couldn't sleep last night. We both slept in … or rather I did, as he sleeps in every day. Before I finally fell asleep, I cleaned out his closet and some drawers. I have begun the process. Dad is unaware as he sleeps. Only Tygee eyes me now and then.

Today I told the boys. We will begin the move shortly. We must be discharged from the facility so to speak … and also tell Hospice. A beginning for the end.

Later in the day I took Dad for a walk in a Home wheelchair. I doubt if he really enjoyed it. No comments, no reaction really. From April 1st onward, he has put one foot ahead of the other, kept himself going mentally, kept LaVerl company, and enjoyed his family each day. That is over now. He did say he needed to have a bowel movement but has had no luck. Must tell Hospice about that. Everything is now geared to his physical state on a daily basis. We are losing sight of dear, sweet Dad.

70

June 9, 2004 (Midnight on Tuesday)

Dear Journal,

It's been a long two days. Couldn't write. I've been crying some. I've been watching President Reagan's funeral on television. That didn't help my mood. He will be laid to rest on Friday at sunset.

His family remains strong during the coverage. I have empathy for Nancy and her sad journey through her husband's decline with Alzheimer's. Dad actually watched some of it. He liked Reagan and said quietly that he was a good president. I wonder if it is true that our loved ones wait for us in heaven. If so, Dad can meet President Reagan, and they can have a good conversation with Mom, my cousin, Sherrie, as well as his dad and mom and brother. He will have many good conversations. I'm the one who will be left alone.

Todd, the Hospice man, is coming by today to check on him. A hospital bed will be delivered to the condo, and Jason brought boxes for packing his things. We started with Dad's books. His collection of Louie L'Amour we packed with care. He spent months going through used bookstores, searching for the missing titles, and then one day he had the full set. A proud day for him … and he read them as he collected them. He also has a start on Zane Gray.

We will have Dad at the condo tonight even if his apartment is not emptied. We have made the proper arrangements with the Home for Dad's leaving. The staff knows of Dad's condition because Hospice told them. We said kind good-byes with sad eyes. I feel that the Home has wanted us to leave, like it was time. Why didn't we? I think I chose to stay because I thought Dad should be with LaVerl and other residents he cared about for as long as possible and keep on with the daily activities that he liked. Or maybe I stayed because of the comfort and security the Home gave to me too. I had others to talk with. I could be a part of something. I had a Home family that was familiar and dependable and distracting.

Last night I lay next to Dad for some time. Told him we were moving. We held hands, and we cried silently together. I have never felt so much love. Its warmth and comfort filled us till we both fell into a peaceful sleep. Tygee snuggled into the space between us. Maybe he cried too. This night I will always hold dear to my heart.

Around 4:00 a.m. I moved to the air mattress. Dad looked so peaceful and calm ... and so little and helpless. I adjusted the oxygen tube on the machine by his bed. I had become so familiar with the hissing sound it made. It was breathing too.

June 13, 2004 (Monday)

Dear Journal,

So tired. So much has gone down since my last entry. We are at the condo now. Although he didn't have that much to move because the furniture belonged to the Home, it still seemed endless. Thursday the boys hauled out the TV and the bookcases. Friday Jeanette came by and cleaned out the last of Dad's stuff from his room. Her help was so appreciated. Since we are out now, I do not want to ever see the place again. When Mom died at Pioneer Hospital, I would drive blocks around it so I wouldn't have to see it for months afterward.

I've been rather disorganized so far. Hospice delivered Dad's hospital bed, and we placed it next to the double windows that look out onto my small patio. I will be able to sit outside, and he will be in view.

On Sunday the boys came by, and Dad sat out on the patio with us for a bit. It seems that he doesn't remember this place, even though he lived here for a while. Yet he will respond correctly to questions about a past event.

Not that he talks. He just responds with a yes or no. Nothing makes sense at this point, not to me either. Hospice also had a commode delivered, and it sits next to the foot of his bed.

The chaplain from Hospice came by to visit. Dad will be given three baths a week by a special person named Cory. Such a young man to be doing this kind of thing. Marie and Todd and other nurses will stop by twice a week or as needed.

Dad spends each day in bed under my watchful eyes and makes trips to the commode. He squeezes my hand and responds to my voice. Then unexpectedly he will try to get out of bed for no particular reason, and I coax him back. I talk with friends and relatives on the phone. I still laugh at things that are funny and carry on with conversations. I am very lonely though, even with all the activity and support around me.

Dad is completely dependent on me, and yet I feel so much like his little girl again.

June 16, 2004 (Wednesday)

Dear Journal,

I know it is Wednesday. My life is so insulated, each day the same as the last and the same as the next. The days of the week are meaningless. I sleep on the couch close to Dad's bed because I want to be near if he tries to get up. And earlier he needed the commode twice because of the suppository given by Marie. I now have her to get more acquainted with. I like her. Mostly it was Todd who came to the home.

I thought I would enjoy my own bed, but I dare not spend too much time upstairs in my bedroom, as it is too far away. I shower and dress there. I take a half hour here or there to watch some television in my den. I would have put Dad's television near his bed, but it holds no interest for him anymore.

I read the Hospice literature today. It says I must release my responsibility for his living any longer. Mentally I did that, but only till an hour or so ago did I do it emotionally. Maybe!

Death. What a *real* event. I feel like I can taste it, touch it, and commune with it. It is all around me. Today I had a strange thought. Wouldn't it be nice if I could just slip in right behind Dad when he walked through death's door? Maybe God wouldn't notice me till I got there. I feel death all around me, so I may as well go now too. Two for one, God.

I slept from 4:00 a.m. to nine o'clock this morning on the couch next to Dad. I read once how a soldier in combat can sleep while he is walking. I have an inkling of how it works now. I was asleep yet awake, always on alert in case he needed me.

Cory gave Dad a bath today. He is so gentle with him, and Dad can feel the kindness in his hands. I just know it. It was a very nice day. Through the windows I notice how beautiful the patio is. I did manage to plant flowers and arrange the outdoor furniture. I even sat outside and read for a bit. God is good. I must believe that.

June 20, 2004 (Father's Day)
Dear Journal,

Things have been hectic since my last entry about four days ago. "How can that be," you say, "with just Dad and me alone here?" Seems I'm always buzzing around and doing something. This caregiving is very time-consuming. I am getting things down into a regular routine. Each day I wash the floor with disinfectant. I straighten out Dad's covers and try to make his bed pretty, even with Tygee to work around. He is glued to Dad's bed except to use his own little commode, which he doesn't seem to need very often. Now and then he leaves to eat a few bites from his dish in the kitchen, and then it's back to Dad's bed.

Verona called me to see if I wanted to be put on the church prayer list. "Why not?" I replied. On

Wednesday, Verona and I went to the Spaghetti Factory for dinner. Again it was great to get out into the everyday world of the living. We had a nice conversation but not about Dad. Jody stayed with him so I could leave.

Marie came on Thursday, and Friday was another bath day with Cory. So the days pass quickly. Of course, Dylan still comes, usually on Mondays and Fridays. Thank God for babysitting my two-year-old grandson.

On Saturday night Pastor O'Donnell and his wife, Cindy, came by to offer their support. Support? I'll take it whatever way it comes. They are very nice people. After Verona put Dad and me on the prayer list, they came by. Dad may have heard us talking, but there was no indication that he realized they were there. We had prayer.

June 23, 2004

Dear Journal,

Can't sleep. Dylan stayed the night here. He is asleep upstairs, while Dad sleeps in front of me. Just think. A week ago today Verona and I went out to eat. It seems like a year ago. Yesterday Verona came by with dinner, which we ate out on the patio. A very nice gesture, and I appreciated it. Jason stopped in, so I made a quick trip to the store for personal items and hurried back.

Dad is in another place. He sleeps most of the time and doesn't respond much. But then there are times when he surprises you with sudden alertness. I'm beginning to wonder what the death itself will be like. I'm not going to spend too much time on that, okay, Journal? I'm sure I can sleep now.

June 27, 2004 (Sunday)

Dear Journal,

Went to church on television. I am sitting on my patio this morning, writing. It is a lovely day. From Dad's Home lanai to my patio—my secret little writing rooms.

I can see Dad sleeping in his bed from here. He looks peaceful, but he is so small and tiny these days. He ate a little more than usual yesterday. I feed him in bed now. Today he was more alert to his surroundings. On Friday various Hospice people passed one another coming and going. Kept him busy. My ex-husband stopped by to see Dad. Many moons ago they saw each other, but even if Dad recognized his voice, there was no communication. He didn't stay long and couldn't talk to Dad. He spoke mostly to me. But I guess he said good-bye. We were married once—something else that seems like a thousand years ago. I will take a break now and have my shower. More later.

(9:00 p.m.) I talked for some time to Dad, sitting on the bed beside him. He squeezes my hand, but there is little strength in it. So I squeeze his. He says a yes or a no and will surprisingly even ask a question now and then. His vision is growing weak.

I never dreamed I would see my father like this. I have learned how to give him his insulin shots, but I'm thinking, *What for?* Maybe I can get a job as a nurse now, but I really don't want to be a shot-giver! One can do many undesirable things when it is necessary though! I'm so glad Dad's bed is in the middle of things so all activity and conversation is around him. Hospice advised this.

He seems content really, and Hospice says he does not seem to be in that much pain, which is a surprise to them. Unsaid is that it may come later. He sleeps deeply, yet at times when I stand over him, his eyes fly open. Who knows how aware he is even though he appears asleep?

My cousins call periodically to see how we are doing. I love them for keeping in touch. The Hospice nurse said the other day that I seemed more peaceful and settled too. She may be right. My life is now very predictable. Day by day it's the same, yet we are moving forward. These days when I am in thought, I recall the man my dad was in my youth. He was rather stocky, and he seemed so strong. I thought he could do anything. I make up my mind that he is still that man. I just have to look beyond what I see lying in bed. *I remember the times I felt his strong arms around me.*

"Here, let me help you," Dad would say, lifting me onto the Case tractor platform. I loved to stand by his side among the gears as we went round after round in the field. Sometimes I would

sit on his lap and steer with his hands gently covering mine.

"Help me move this," Dad would say. Then with each of us grasping the side of a heavy board, we would place it against the barn to brace the door that was now sagging to the side. "Hafta fix this one day." I would nod in agreement.

One early cold Spring day Mom and I looked out the kitchen window and saw Dad carrying a newborn calf toward the house. "It's not gonna make it," Dad said sadly, entering the front shed of the house. "She licked it into the icy water of the pond after birth."

Under Mom's prompting, we rubbed, stroked, and talked the calf back to life. The heavy blankets and warmth of the shed also helped.

"Told you so," Mom said, laughing, "I knew we could save it." Then Dad lifted the calf into his arms to take it back to its mama.

Dad was always lifting something, pulling something, or moving something. Often he was fixing something. To see him bending over machinery with greasy hands or attaching the plow to the tractor with a few grunts or groans was a familiar sight. Physical activity was the name of the game each and every day.

Most of all I remember him pulling me into his arms, hugging me, and with a small smile, saying, "You're a great help."

June 28, 2004 (Monday)

Dear Journal,

Today the chaplain for Hospice stopped in and had prayer with Dad and me. We are born helpless children, and we die helpless children. I'm grateful for all the days in between. That's part of what the chaplain said. And then something about my father living to be old. Some people are denied that. He also said that living through the death of someone we love can be a great learning experience.

So what am I learning? The way I see it, life is a school. A lesson learned here, another there. Some are quite easy, and it goes up from there to difficult to seemingly impossible. We throw in a mixture of rebellion, unfinished or undone homework, denial of the lesson altogether, and at times we may try to get someone else to do our lesson for us. All in all we keep going. There is no way out. We've got the length of our days doing life-school work. Now that is the way I see things today, Journal. Do you not agree?

June 30, 2004 (Wednesday)
Dear Journal,

The morning of the last day of June. This is going down as the last June of my life as well. What? I can't believe I wrote that. I just reread it a couple of times. I know now, beyond any doubt, how much of this journey of Dad's is mine also. I've personalized it, haven't I? Where he is—I am! Where he goes—I go!

Marie stopped by to check on him. Says all is going as expected. I knew she would say that. All medications are gone now, except medication for pain. I have morphine and also the marijuana capsules. Maybe I should take a few.

Marie and I have a talk. She offers comfort and explanations of what is going on and what to expect. It helps so much. They are like family now, knowing my Dad as well as I do at this stage of his life. We say good-bye with a hug. I now welcome them with all my heart.

Today is Dylan day. He is taking his nap in his upstairs bed, and Dad sleeps downstairs. I know Dad is aware of him and oftentimes reaches out to him. Dylan will go over to the bed to say "hi" as he peers into Dad's face. He also pets Tygee, who is usually sleeping as well. Then off he goes again to see what else is in the house that might offer adventure.

I must go now. Time to feed Dylan and me. Dad isn't interested in eating today.

JULY

July 3, 2004 (Saturday)

Dear Journal,

Wow! July is here. I don't recall June. Maybe not April or May either. Summer is out there, but I only experience it on the patio except for brief trips to a store. Wow, July. What will it hold? Dad's sugar this morning was thirty-five. Luckily he did drink the orange juice I offered him immediately, and he had some spoonfuls of cereal and milk. Later it read 103.

Todd advised me yesterday that Dad could slip away at any time, so don't be surprised. Of course, I think that would be wonderful. I know it's time … for him and for me. The people of Hospice tell me that they are amazed that he hasn't passed yet. That is such a great word—passed. Don't you think? They are also amazed that he seems to be in no real pain. Unlike others they have attended to.

Oh, I forgot to mention Anna, the harp lady. She stopped by yesterday to play for Dad. When they suggested it, I said Dad wasn't into music that much, especially harps! But they seemed to think it would be nice, so I agreed. We took Dad's blood pressure before she started. Then she began. It was truly heavenly music. I relaxed on the sofa and listened gratefully. Dad, seemingly unaware, lay quietly. When she had finished about a half hour later, we took his blood pressure again, and it had gone down. She told me this happened often. Unbelievable. She is a lovely lady and may return.

I also forgot to mention Tygee. Really mention him. By that, I mean his behavior. When someone from Hospice shows up, Tygee immediately comes to life. As they examine Dad, Tygee is poking and prodding his nose against them as if to get their attention. When they pause for a second, he stares into their eyes and meows this strange meow. It's as though he is saying, "Do something. Do something." Many times the Hospice person attending to Dad has teared up. They sense Tygee's desperation. They call him an unusual cat.

Tygee and me—we are the two who are suffering the most. We are buddies in this, bonded forever. What will he do after dad *passes*? What will I do? Go with Dad? Or go soon after? Yesterday I did the usual washing of the floor and taking care of the damned commode. I cleaned, cleaned, cleaned. Anything that passed in front of me received a good wiping, scrubbing, or polishing. Cleaning is good, and so are the calls from family and friends.

If I pause too long, I can see Mom's face, and I miss her so much. I push her away. But only so far-- just far enough so that I can see her watching me, yet the pain isn't intolerable. She is the one who taught me to clean. Bet she never thought I would get obsessed by it though. Soon I will be missing Dad too as well as her. I'm beginning to feel the loss of him now bit by bit as I observe him slipping away from me--from his place in the world. You know, our place in the world is much more important than we realize. We must make the most of it. Hmm, never thought about it much before. Our place in the world— I have a place, and I take up my space. I choose what to do with it.

Yesterday Marlon Brando died. That is earth-shattering to me, or somewhat anyway. My favorite actor can't just leave his place and space in this world. I actually cried for a few minutes. He went through his school of life. From what I've heard or read, it wasn't always easy. Funny how one can miss a celebrity. Marlon Brando was my personal rebel. He did it for me through his movies since I never had the courage to become an out-and-out rebel myself!

I'm rambling, but that is okay. I feel an urgency to keep writing. So on to a little story about Dad and Mom. Each New Year, we watched the ball come down in Times Square. After we had watched the special programs that told us of the major happenings throughout the previous year, Dad would say, "Yup, I don't know if we'll make it through another year. The world can't keep going like this."

To which Mom would reply, "You said that last New Year's Eve and the one before that, and we're still here." Then we'd laugh.

She would look across him to me as if we were sharing a special knowledge. As a child, I wasn't quite sure how to digest this little scenario. Should I look forward to a good year or a bad one? Aren't memories of childhood precious?

Mom and Dad had such different tastes. He loved Gary Cooper. He told me to observe how he rode in a saddle in a movie. You could tell he was a true cowboy. No acting required. Dad loved Tom Mix, the silent screen star. To think that Dad watched silent movies and then moved on to talkies doesn't register with me. He had a little crush on Betty White, who had a series on TV. And more recently he enjoyed her on the *Golden Girls*.

From Mom I learned to love Bette Davis—movies like *Moulin Rouge*—and yes, Marlon Brando. She introduced me to Brook Benton and Joe Stafford. Dad's favorite songs were "My Darling Nellie Gray," "Home on the Range," and "Little Old Sod Shanty on my Claim."

Dad only reached eighth grade but had a keen interest in history and was really curious with the Mayan ruins in Mexico. And he saw almost all of them while we traveled the Yucatan Peninsula on a recent tour. I wish he would have traveled to Africa, which he talked about often.

I recall the many car trips we took around the United States.

"This is the Continental Divide," my father would explain as we drove through Montana. I would look out the window at the same river and forest that we had been seeing for miles. If the Continental Divide was there, I certainly couldn't see it. "All the water on that side of the line runs into the Pacific Ocean. All the water on the other side runs into the Atlantic." I knew what he told me was important, but it wasn't clear to me why.

My father taught me where specific rivers originated, what other rivers ran into them, where they came out to the ocean, why certain crops were grown in certain places, why farmers did things differently in different parts of the country, how high the mountains were, how deep the lakes. I learned about mountain ranges, valleys and plateaus. He'd point in a certain direction and say that if we went straight across the land as the crow flies, we'd come to a city. Instead we had to follow the road and travel curves and bends that took up extra time. I learned why roads were laid in certain patterns and why towns possibly were where they were. All these facts I learned without really being aware of the fact of learning. My father just talked about such things as he drove. Perhaps he was talking to himself as much as to my mother and me.

July 4, 2004 (Sunday)

Dear Journal,

Wow, the day for fireworks. I sat on the patio under the umbrella early this morning listening to it rain. It's like I can hear individual drops hit the top—plop, plop, plop. So relaxing. I can, of course, see that Dad is still asleep.

I forgot to mention that in the afternoon yesterday Don and Bernice from church came by. They now live in Florida and were home for a visit with family. We had a very nice visit, and then we stood by Dad's bed to include him in prayer. I am grateful that they came by. I've known them for years and worked part-time in their business off and on.

Then later in the day we had a cookout on the patio. Jody and Jeanette handled the details. Jason talked to Dad. I scurried around. It all turned out very nice. Dad doesn't get out of his bed, but I'm sure he's aware of all of us buzzing around him as we move back and forth and then onto the patio. We even set off a few safe fireworks just outside the building area on the nearest street, although Dad missed that. And so we had our Fourth of July in 2004. The last Independence Day Dad will ever know.

Now they are gone. I'm too tired to cry, but I want to. I sit quietly on the sofa next to Dad and listen to him breath. It fills the room.

July 5, 2004 (Monday)

Dear Journal,

I've been lying next to Dad and crying. He's asleep and not very responsive to my touch. I touch his face, and here comes Tygee with his little paw joining in. We want a human reaction. A laugh, a cry … anything that says he is with us. Tygee's devotion touches my heart deeply, and I reach out to pet him. He deserves a medal for loyalty.

Earlier in the day around noon Dad needed to use the commode. I always know because he begins to get restless and tries to move to a sitting position. This is one endeavor that he seems to come alive for. I rush to his side and help him get out of bed to support his whole weight, which is nothing now. Then we move in unison to the commode to help him with his little project. For some reason this time didn't work out quite right, and I almost lost my balance. I managed to regain our stance to prevent our falling to the floor.

In an unguarded, uncontrolled moment I was instantly angry. How many times did I have to do this? Why couldn't he be a bit more cooperative? Couldn't he at least stand for a little bit? I can't remember my exact words. Something like, "Can't you at least help me or walk a little ways?" Maybe I said, "Damn it." At any rate the look of surprise in his sad eyes hit me like a ton of bricks. Total disbelief at my anger. At that moment, he was very much aware. Aware of me. And I became sadly very aware of me as well.

The room was silent during the next moments as we continued with our commode ritual. Then he gratefully slid back into bed and went immediately asleep.

Who was I? How could I be so terrible? I've lost it. I'm mean? If I were a Catholic, would I go to confession? I bet I wouldn't be forgiven.

After I thought it through, I realized I truly had lost it. After months of stress I finally lost it over a very small incident. I must apologize to him when I lay next to him, which I do now for an hour or two near my bed time. I just talk and talk. Now I must add an apology.

Tygee has changed his ritual. Every now and then he jumps off the bed and walks around it yowling. A God-awful yowl. After a few minutes of that, he then jumps back on the bed and usually settles now on Dad's chest. Tonight is turning into a long night, and so I choose to write. Just me and Tygee getting through the night with our loved one. God have mercy on us.

July 6, 2004 (Tuesday)

Dear Journal,

Dad made it through the night. Sometimes it seemed he wasn't breathing. If I remember from the Hospice literature, this happens toward the end. Hospice is scheduled to come today. I pray for energy to get through this day. When I thought that Dad might not make it last night, I felt desperate to help him see the morning light. Now that he has, I have to remind myself that he hasn't really gained anything, and sadly neither have I.

I did apologize as I lay next to him. I hope it registered, and he heard it. I regret my behavior, although I now understand it.

Marie told me that Hospice found my dad quite interesting. For one thing, he just seemed resigned from the moment he was told he was going to die. Unlike some people, I guess his acceptance seemed out of the ordinary to them. They also have marveled that he is not gone already. He just lingers. And so they visit, talk to him, check him out with Tygee's help, give me words of encouragement and instruction. Then they give me a hug and leave. I have come to love them all. Who needs Hospice? I do!

July 7, 2004 (Wednesday)

Dear Journal,

I know it is Wednesday. I do glance at my calendar once in a while. Otherwise, I would have no idea. Today I fed Dad ice cream because of a very low sugar reading. So I thought ice cream might help. Does it really matter? I must discuss this with Hospice next time they come.

The day goes by with no real change in our routine. I clean and disinfect the floor once again, clean the commode, and straighten Dad's blankets over his body. He sleeps, and I have a bite to eat. Nothing tastes good to me now either.

(3:00 a.m.) Dad just woke up and glanced toward the couch to see if I was there. I smile at him. Of course I'm here. He seems very much aware suddenly and wants to talk. Very clearly he tells me that he is going on a trip. I ask, "Where to?"

"I don't know, but I could see them. There are people waiting for me to come." I ask if he recognized anyone. "No, but I think I know them. I know I do." He gives me a big smile. I haven't seen that in a long time. And then he falls back to sleep.

I am left to ponder. Marie told me about this type of thing. They experience this many times in different ways with people who are dying. Marie says she could tell many such stories herself. I am happy for Dad that he had this experience. It made *him very happy.* And me as well.

It dawns on me that I can hardly remember the day when Dad wasn't lying in a bed. It's about a month now that we left the Home. That day seems unreal. Today seems unreal. Actually since April 1, nothing has seemed real. I have become an unreal me. Dad is the only reality. I feel now a sort of numbness crawling over my body very, very slowly.

July 10, 2004 (Saturday)

Dear Journal,

Each time I write, I notice that it seems a thousand years have passed since my last entry. It just slides away and turns into the distant past. I have not read one word of what I have written so far. I have a feeling it will be a long while before I can even touch this journal. I must find a safe place to keep it till then. I know for certain, though, that one day I will have an overwhelming desire to open it and read.

Todd and a companion were here yesterday. As they enter, they shake their heads to see that Dad is still among us. Most of all they cannot believe he seems in so little pain and remains calm. Marie told me it may be because he is not shut away and he feels a part of us even if he seems to sleep most of the time. He shows no anxiety or irritability. Dr. Cato has now told Hospice to take away the insulin. My days of being a shot-giver are over. The boys continue to stop periodically. I can see the sadness in their eyes as they look at him and then at Tygee and me.

Dad can still swallow a little water or juice, but he is coughing more. He says words that I cannot decipher, and I am frustrated by that. I so want to know what he is trying to say. I hold his hand and give him a kiss. I tell him I love him. Today he mouthed the words, "I love you too." Now *that* I understood.

I call his bed the crying field now. Only to myself, of course. Sometimes I want to approach his bed and find that he is gone. But no, I want to be present when he leaves me. The desire to go with him comes back more and more. I don't want to cover this same ground again. Just let me go on this journey now. I'll sneak in behind him some way.

It dawns on me suddenly, maybe Dad isn't leaving because he knows I want to come along. Maybe he feels he has to let me know somehow, that I must stay behind and can't find a way. Maybe that was what I couldn't make out.

Despite the sadness, I feel good. A little numb but calm. I am finding great comfort and strength being alone with him. It has come over me the last few days. We can do this ourselves. Just the two of us and Tygee. My cat spends a lot of time sleeping on my bed upstairs. She comes down to eat and use her litter box. Sometimes she will jump on Dad's bed as if to talk for a bit with Tygee. They both make cat noises. But then she is off, leaving us behind to cope.

July 11, 2004

Dear Journal,

It's Sunday. Another church day. I will worship in my own way just as Dad has done his whole life. Like him, I feel close to God when I'm in nature. When I see geese migrating, when I see a seed break through the soil, when I hear the crack of thunder, when I hear a coyote howl--I know there is a God. I washed Dad's face and hands. It's my job when it's not bath day. This morning he ate a good portion of Jell-O and then went back to sleep.

Looking past Dad out the window, I can see that it is a wonderful, warm, sunny day. Most days I spend an hour or more sitting in my favorite chair on the patio. And there I write. Sometimes I write after dark under the lamp next to the entry door.

I find comfort especially when I write at night. Maybe it's the stillness. Everyone sleeps except me. I find that strangely captivating. Just me, my journal, and the night.

July 12, 2004 (Monday)

Dear Journal,

Real. Unreal. It's like the only way I will know that this experience truly happened is when I look for Dad and I won't find him anywhere. I won't hear his familiar voice or see him walking across the room. Is that when you realize that your loved one is actually gone?

I'm in a haze, a fog, a dream. But he is here, even though he is not here. Todd said Dad did not fit the usual profile. His blood pressure is still okay, and his pulse is as well. But Todd has noticed a change. He told me not to worry about feeding him anymore. When close to death, a person knows he does not want food. It's in their best interest not to try to force it. Also, it could go into his lungs.

I'm running out of things to do to make myself think I am doing some good. So I rearrange

his covers, give Tygee a couple of pats. I give both
a quick kiss and tell them that I love them. Dylan
was here today. Dad did reach out and touched
Dylan's head in response to Dylan's calling him
papa. Dylan was playing around the bed. Dylan,
being two, seems to think it is normal to have
an old man lying in a bed in the living room. I call
that a blessing.

Thank God he lived to enjoy his only
great-grandson even for approximately two short
years. Dad loved to show him off to the other
residents of the Home.

Just received a phone call from Andrew in
Wisconsin. He is the husband of Esther. Dad's
family tree that I haven't truly understood so far.
Anyway, he is sending me a letter written by Dad's
father when Dad was a kid. In it he expresses his
sadness that my dad lost an eye in a pitchfork
accident on the farm. They took the train to
Minneapolis, thinking they could save the eye, but
the trip took too long. Dad even learned to fly with
one eye as an adult, and his instructor was
impressed by how he still could make such good

landings and line things up so well. Dad never really talked about it. It just became a part of him.

July 12, 2004 (Tuesday)

Dear Journal,

I now track the days simply to know. It doesn't actually matter. But hey, Journal, I'm writing a journal. Anna, the harp lady, came by again. She played. We relaxed into the beauty of the moment which lasted about a half an hour. She again checked his pulse before and after, and it had gone down.

Jason came by to watch Dad while I went for a much-needed massage. Wonderful, wonderful. When I arrived home, Marie was there. Together we changed Dad's sheets, which is getting harder to do because Dad cannot cooperate any longer. He is wearing diapers now. Since Todd couldn't make it, we bathed him and changed his T-shirt. Learned the trick of cutting his shirt down the middle for easy removal.

Lilly, a Hospice counselor, came by, and we had a nice visit under difficult circumstances. I felt comforted, understood, and accepted no matter what. A good feeling. Hospice has become my lifeline, my connection to people who know every little inch of what is going down. "It is very close now," she says.

They leave, and it is suddenly very quiet. I turn on the radio to soft music, which I often do. I think about something good to eat. But I know from experience if I make it, I will be full after two bites and maybe have a stomachache. If I were addicted to drugs or cigarettes, I would maybe be in big trouble by now.

The massage has made me tired, and so I move to the couch for a quick nap after I gaze down at Dad. He doesn't even take oxygen anymore and can swallow just trickles of water. We sponge out his mouth when it gets dry.

July 13, 2004 (Wednesday)

Dear Journal,

It is overcast today, which matches my mood perfectly. Just cleaned Dad's mouth and washed his face. Pastor O'Donnell and Roy Trotter from church stopped by. They did an anointing for Dad and then me as well. I was comforted and felt an overwhelming peace in their presence. We sat at the table and talked very quietly about a memorial service. Nothing was decided definitely, but for the first time the subject was approached. I guess we need pastors to steer us down the road when we can't see it.

After a memorial service, perhaps at the condo, we will take Dad home to the farm to be buried in the neighborhood cemetery with a graveside ceremony. He will be cremated. He will be home.

The kids and I talked this over. Dad never did say what he wanted. It was just understood from other conversations from years before.

Lars and Lisa called. Andrew from Wisconsin called to confirm that I had gotten the letter. Patty in Seattle called.

It's like this is really over, except Dad keeps breathing.

July 14, 2004 (Thursday)

Dear Journal,

Yes, I am still writing. It grounds me, makes me know I am alive. Dad isn't moving anymore. Just lies quietly and breathes heavily and deep. I sit close to him periodically and talk of everyday things—the farm, the boys, Dylan, and even the weather.

Nancy from church was here and delivered a beautiful floral bouquet. That brightened my spirits. We sat and talked for a while. She asked if I had emotionally released Dad yet. I said I thought so. Then she told me to actually tell him he could go. He needs to hear that. Sometimes dying people need to know that they can leave. I hadn't even thought of that. It made perfect sense. He has to know that I will be fine without him, that I will be strong, and that I can make it on my own.

"Pick a time to do it and think of what you want to say," Nancy continued.

"I will," I said tearfully. We hugged, and she was gone.

"First I'm going to tell him that I understand he must go alone and I can't come with," I said softly into the quiet room. I have my own journey to make that belongs only to me. I'll tell him tonight when it's dark and when all will be more quiet and still. It had to be done … for him and for me.

And so … I did it. It is too painful to go over all that I said. I expressed my love for him and told him I would be fine without him. I would take care of Tygee. Not to worry about the farm. I talked about our history together, shared experiences of my childhood. I talked about Mom. I don't know how long it took. Time stood still. I repeated that it was fine for him to go. I would have to come later.

I held him in my arms, crying. He didn't respond, but I knew he heard me. I released him and went to the couch and fell into a deep sleep.

July 15, 2004
Dear Journal,

Dad is still here. I have my morning coffee, sit next to him on the couch. I see my father so thin and frail, hanging on to each breath, and then he hardly breathes at all. I know it will be soon now. He will leave us at last.

Then I remembered something—a story he told me about a pact he had made with his brother, Carl, many years before. One day, as young men, they were talking about death, the afterlife, and they wondered if it were possible to communicate with the dead. According to Dad, his brother said, "Let's make a pact. Whoever of us goes first, will, if possible, get in touch with the one left behind. Let's shake on it." And they did.

Over the years Dad would retell that story for one reason or another and then add with a little laugh, "Haven't heard a word."

Dad and I must make the same pact. I sit next to him on the bed and remind him of the pact between him and his brother. Then I tell him we must have the same agreement. I shake his hand. There is no strength in it now. Not even a squeeze.

I tell him I love him and say a little prayer for both of us. All is quiet and still except for soft music coming from the radio. Both cats are lying on Dad's bed at the same moment. Strange that my cat joined us!

July 16, 2004 (11:00 p.m. on Friday)

Dear Journal,

It is finished! It's over for Dad. He slipped through death's door—and I'm still here.

Jody had come over to stay the night. He went upstairs to sleep. I lay by Dad, holding him in my arms. Again his breathing seemed to fill the room. It seemed to be the only sound in the whole wide world. I was extremely tired. So tired it seemed I couldn't even think or feel anything anymore. I fell into a deep sleep next to him.

Sometime during the night I woke up with a jolt. I was in a most uncomfortable position. I had to get to the couch somehow. Sleep. I needed sleep. I remember almost falling onto the couch and nothing more. Just blessed sleep.

(5:00 a.m.) Something woke me up. Not a noise, not any movement in the house. I just woke up like a light switch being turned on. And I knew. I didn't want to look, to see, but I had to.

I turned to Dad, moved toward him. I touched his hand. He was gone.

I called up the stairs to Jody. He stumbled downstairs, half awake, and almost ran to Dad. After a quick examination he knew it too. We both kissed him and then called Hospice. Jody called Jason. Tygee moved from the foot of the bed up to Dad's chest and buried his nose in his neck. He knew too. It's strange, but I swear I could read it in his eyes.

We moved to the patio and sat at the table in the early light, in quiet contemplation. Just Jody and me. Then unbelievably a strange cat appeared. A beautiful gold cat, with eyes full of divine wisdom, jumped on the patio table and seemed to offer comfort. We had never seen that cat before. Jody and I stared at each other in wonder. Where did it come from? And why? Then it vanished as unexpectedly as it had appeared!

Marie from Hospice arrived and did a quick examination of Dad. She offered us comfort and support. It felt good to have her there. I felt relief that it was over and also deep, gut-wrenching pain.

Everything was happening too fast. Suddenly the Deseret Funeral Home was there. Where did they come from so soon? I guess Marie called them. I didn't want them there. They were such an intrusion. But we had no choice. Dad had to go. He had to actually leave the house. Dead or alive, I didn't want him to go. He was supposed to lay in that bed forever. I had grown accustomed to it. It was a part of my life.

Activity was going on around me. Jason arrived. Two men and Marie were talking. I watched as they fussed around Dad. I felt detached from it all. Jody, Jason, and I said our last good-byes to Dad. I removed Tygee from Dad's chest and held him. Like in a dream, I watched Dad being zipped inside a body bag. He was put on a gurney, and they took him away. They just took him away as if they owned him. Beneath my pain I felt anger.

Marie talked to us some more. Don't remember any words. Then she left. The empty bed stared at us. Tygee jumped back on the bed and began to pace back and forth. I again picked him up. There was a knock on the door. It was

Alpine Equipment. Within a half hour everything that pertained to Dad was gone, from the oxygen supply to his bed. Not one shred of evidence remained. They offered their sympathy, and then they were gone.

The door closed behind them. Tygee jumped from my arms and circled around the area where the bed had been. It was happening too fast for him too. I had to do something so I carried him upstairs to my bed and left him there. Suddenly he seemed too drained to care as he slumped into the covers.

When I came downstairs, Jody was in the process of rearranging the furniture. Soon the living room looked like my living room again. It didn't look right. It didn't feel right.

How could it all be over? I recalled that I had experienced a sudden jolt of realization that Dad was probably gone when I stumbled in a stupor from his bed to the couch during the night. I vaguely recalled that he had rolled away from me like a dead weight when I left the bed.

It hadn't happened right. I wanted to be there for him when he drew his last breath. To be holding his hand. To be aware. No, it hadn't gone the way I had expected, but I was so tired. More tired than I could remember ever being. I felt no energy, just weakness.

I had given him my permission to leave us, but I never expected him to go when I was asleep. Of course, Dad would do it this way. He would think it best for all of us to just go away on his own. No reason to make a big fuss over it. Dad's gone. It's over.

It seemed like the day had two parts. The first part is about them taking Dad away. The second part is about people. Verona stopped in to give comfort and support and actually offered her home for a memorial celebration. Nancy stopped in with more flowers. In the afternoon the boys and I went to the funeral home to sign papers and make arrangements. Jason had picked up Dylan, so he went too. It made things easier, more normal. We ate at a cafe. I guess I ate something. The Jackson family came by later in the evening, and so did Pastor O'Donnell and Cindy.

At midnight the house was quiet. I told the boys that I would be fine alone. No need for them to stay the night. I needed some solitude. I sat quietly in the dim light of the patio and tried to recall the day. Had I taken care of business? Yes, I had contacted my out-of-state relatives and friends. Yes, we had made proper arrangements for Dad's cremation. Yes, we knew the memorial celebration would be at Verona's. The important things had been taken care of.

It was done. I could relax. I turned off the porch light. I sat for a long time, observing the small portion of the night sky I could see from my little corner of the world. A few stars flickered at me, their light faint as it filtered through the lights of the city. Suddenly I longed for the night sky of my youth, the farm. The stars there were so close that one could touch them. I know Dad must have longed many times for that too. I sat for a long time in my comfortable chair with Dad's presence still around me.

April Fool's Day now seemed like a thousand years ago. I have traveled a long way

115

since then. Me and my daddy—we journeyed together. And then it ended by us taking different forks in the road. I didn't get to go with him after all. But that's just fine. We each have our own vanishing point. But the moment will come when we'll be together again.

Okay, Dad?

Caregiver

I don't know how I make it through—
The highs, the lows
The ups, the downs.
But
Most of all—
I don't know how I travel
Through the standing still.
Truth is—
I die a thousand times,
Sigh a thousand sighs,
Ask a thousand whys,
Yet like a friend,
I cannot greet—
Time knocks

Waits—
And without a response,
Time slips away from me.
My time to dream, to feel,
To wonder, to be—
My time to think, to ponder,
To laugh, to see,
Taken away for eternity.
At first time trickles, then gains some speed—
Rushes into gullies, cracks unseen,
Like a river, it rushes to an unknown place
To lose itself in a bottomless sea.
Time,

My time—
Isn't meant to be.

Time, so precious,
Time, so small,
Time, so fleeting,
Time on call.
Yet for me—
Time is not.
It will come never.
That's the struggle
For a caring,
Gentle,
Loving
Caregiver.

by Evie Stiehl-Brunner

MEMORIES OF UNCLE HIENEI

It is an "event" in life when one has memories at the age of about five years old. Such a memory was created for me by Hienei Stiehl at his farm. I was with my mother at the farm when Uncle Hienei must have seen my boredom in doing nothing. He came out with a small steel toy car which I can still picture in my mind. He tied a string on the front axle so I could pull it around. As most families, we were of little means, and that toy car really made my day. It was my Uncle Hienei that made it that way. I always remembered how his caring way turned my day into one of great joy.

I also have a memory of my first ever plane ride as a little boy in Uncle Hienei's own plane on his farm. Uncle Hienei was always such a fun, caring, and giving person to be around.

Even as a very young child I became aware of, and realized, his true character.

Over the following fifty plus years, visiting with Uncle Hienei, I felt privileged to know such a man as he was. Always a positive experience as his soft spoken personality emitted a kindness for everyone he encountered. I was proud he was my Uncle as his reputation in all areas of life was spotless. He was a humble man with strength in many aspects.

– Larry Iverson (nephew)

~

Every year since I was five, my dad and I would go back to the homestead in North Dakota for a week or two period. Those two weeks were so memorable to me as I was growing up, and still is, now at age seventy.

Hienei, Hilda and Evie were like the family that I never had. The few weeks seemed like I lived with them for years. (We'd see one another two or three times a year.) It was so much fun and lots of laughs.

The few years on our visits, Hienei would want to take me up flying in his airplane. He always asked me if I wanted to ride the bucking horse. Thinking he was talking about horseback riding, I'd say yes. So up and down he'd dive the plane until I said that I was getting sick, and that I really wanted to ride a real horse.

So many happy memories of the trips to town, visiting, shopping, and watching the men sitting outside the stores playing checkers and card games waiting for the women to get through shopping. I remember moving cattle from the South pasture to the North pasture, branding cattle, and horseback riding. I lived the country life which I loved.

One year I remember, we all decided we were going to go on a long trip to Alaska! So Hienei loaded up the car and Evie, me, my dad, Uncle Hienei and Aunt Hilda headed to Canada, which was beautiful. Hienei had us girls playing word games, counting Beetle cars, and counting the deer we saw, to keep us entertained. Then Evie and I decided to write up signs and put them in the back window of the car. (Alaska or bust.) We'd ask questions to the drivers behind us, and some of them would put up signs answering. We were probably driving Hienei crazy with all the fuss we were making. He kept telling us to settle down.

One time we were going through a town and a police office tried to stop Hienei. Hienei kept driving, thinking it was us girls pounding on the window with our signs. After stopping and talking to the policeman, Hienei told us girls "no more signs." He was really ticked at us.

We got as far as Dawson Creek and decided that we would return home. The roads were getting really bad as they were not paved and it was raining a lot. It put a huge toll on the car. Even though we turned around we had a good time.

Hienei was a devoted father and uncle. I would do anything for his family. His life was an inspiration to all that really knew him. A simple man, he stood for goals, he stood for goals worth the effort to achieve them. He was conservative with investments but was willing to take risks for a good outcome.

He was not flashy, but solid. His cherished life will be sorely missed. His advice and mild mannered personality will forever be in my memories.

– Linda (Stiehl) Kennedy (niece)

~

Growing up in a farming community among the Iverson aunts, uncles and cousins was truly special as we shared holidays and special occasions. As we've gotten older, we cousins have enjoyed sharing memories of this time in our lives ... many of them concerning Uncle Hienei's farm. There was always something special to do there.

One Christmas he just knew that Evie wanted a train set ... so, of course, he got her one. He set it up on the dining room table and we kids stood there, at eye level, watching it go round and round the track with lights and whistles. I imagined myself taking a trip on that very train. We all enjoyed it, but I think Uncle Hienei enjoyed it more because he got to be the conductor.

Another fun experience was when he took us

flying. He was the only farmer I knew who had his own airplane and landing field. We would fly over the coulee's and farmland and again I would pretend I was on a special trip.

After our family left our farm and moved to town, I remember a time the Stiehl's came to visit. Uncle Hienei, Evie and I went for a walk in the neighborhood and as we passed one of the homes, I boldly told them that German's lived there. Uncle Hienei said, "They do? What do they look like?" I couldn't describe them, but told him they talked funny. We went along with my story and we discussed Germans on our walk. I just assumed he was Norwegian like all the Iversons, and of course, he then told me he was a German too. We laughed about this a lot as the years went by!

After leaving North Dakota, getting married and living in California, I enjoyed several visits with Uncle Hienei and Aunt Hilda and shared more good times. Thanks for the memories.

– Janice (Iverson) Mayfield (niece)

~

When I think of Uncle Hienei, the aroma
of instant Postum permeates my space and I can see
him ... sitting in the kitchen at the end of the chrome
table in his bib overalls, drinking Postum, his
glasses perched on top of his head. Uncle Hienei
was a kind, caring and gentle man with an
infectious chuckle. He was very passionate about
his family and farming. He would be up early and
out in the fields from sunup to sundown during
planting or harvest time. In the evenings you
could find him in his shop sharpening tools or
working on farm equipment. Oh yes, he liked to
have fun but only when all the work was done. He
was a man of his word and expected nothing less
from his friends.

One of the biggest treats was going for a ride
in his airplane. Back in those days very few people
flew let alone had their own plane so I thought he
was someone special. He was always happy to take
us nieces and nephews for rides. We thought we
were pretty cool. He would also let us sit in
the plane and we could pretend we were flying, just
don't run the battery down.

Years went by and lives moved on but when I would come back for a visit it was always fun to meet in town for lunch, catch up on news and listen to him chuckle.

Yes, Uncle Hienei was one of a kind and kind he was. Loved by many!

– *Joyce (Iverson) Carter (niece)*

~

About the Author

Evie Stiehl-Brunner spent her childhood days on the family farm located in northwestern North Dakota. In a granary converted into a one-room schoolhouse located a few miles from her home, she went from first through eighth grade.

At present she divides her time between her home in Salt Lake City and her beloved childhood home on the North Dakota prairie. She truly can go home again, as the original farmhouse still beckons her to return. Because of her rural background, she has a deep love for the land and all animals.

Family life always comes first. She and her family share many happy times together. She and her grandson especially enjoy participating in karate.

She has also published a childhood memoir, *Hardscrabble Girl.*

Evie Stiehl-Brunner   Vanishing Point: A Caregiver's Memoir

CPSIA information can be obtained
at www.ICGtesting.com
Printed in the USA
FSHW011953020519
57804FS